Return

Poems

Leo Aylen

*for Simon
with best wishes
Leo Aylen
29.9.88*

Sidgwick & Jackson
London

By the same author

POETRY

Discontinued Design (Venture Press 1969)
I, Odysseus (Sidgwick & Jackson 1971)
Sunflower (Sidgwick & Jackson 1976)

CHILDREN'S OPERA

Gods of the North (Chappell & Co. 1980)
(a series of three children's operas based on three Norse legends: The Apples of Youth; The Giants of Ice and Snow; The God of the Sun. Music by Annette Battam.)

CRITICISM

Greek Tragedy and the Modern World (Methuen 1964)

TRAVEL

Greece for Everyone (Sidgwick & Jackson 1976)

First Published in Great Britain in 1980
by Sidgwick & Jackson Limited
Copyright © Leo Aylen 1980

Reprinted October 1980
3rd Impression 1982
4th Impression 1984
5th Impression 1985
ISBN 0 283 98600 X

Printed in Great Britain by
The Chameleon Press Limited, London SW18
for Sidgwick & Jackson Limited
1 Tavistock Chambers, Bloomsbury Way
London WC1A 2SG

Contents

There are a number of people – English, Welsh, Scots, French, American – without whom many of these poems would not have happened, and to whom this book could be dedicated. But they will forgive me, I hope, if I dedicate it instead to the people of Zululand, that beautiful hill country where I was born, but which I left as a baby and revisited for the first time only recently. My father had gone out there as an Anglican priest, and was then elected Bishop. He did not marry until he was in his fifties, and so I never knew him in his prime. I thought that I might discover something of him as a younger man in Zululand. I had no idea that I would meet such plentiful and vigorous recollections of him. I was regaled with stories of his younger days, some of which must have happened over fifty years ago. There were so many people – on the roads, in the hills, in the middle of suddenly flooding rivers – from whom I received so much that any list of names must be inadequate. This book is for the people of Zululand, and for the people I met in so many different places and circumstances; for Laduma Madela, the great sangoma; King Zwelithini; three bishops – Lawrence Zulu, Alphaeus Zulu, and, if I may include a Swazi, Bernard Mkhabela; the priests Philip Mbatha, Edward Dhlamlenze, Paul Sibiya, Peter Biyela, Jacob Dhlamini, Zeb Mtetwa and Archdeacon Dhladhla; for Prince Gideon Zulu, Princess Aylen Zulu, and the Princess who works in the Mahlabathini bottle store; for Mr and Mrs Nxumalo, Sibusiso Bengu, Thandanani Mkize, Lizzie Mqwebu, Allina Ndebele, Cyprian Mcwango, Beauty Jiane, Fikile, Siphiwo, Robert, Bathulise, Thuli; for the nuns of Twasana who gave me the Zulu name of Sibusiso which means "blessing"; for the poet who interrupted an Inkatha rally to shout a modern praise poem; for the man I found beaten up at the roadside and drove to hospital on Christmas Eve; for the man who tried to give me the huge sum of 10 rand – which can be a family's monthly cash income – because I had done him the honour of attending his party. It is for Zisizeni, Vukani, E. D. A. and all who work for them and for the other community development groups, who are slowly – very slowly – changing society, not through revolution, but by planting orchards, breeding chicken, making baskets and constructing water-wheels out of broken tractor parts. It is for all their families, whom if I named individually I should run out of paper. It is for the white Zulus, and the non-white white Zulus: Paul, Anita, Bill, Pam, Peter, Rosemary, another Bill, another Rosemary, Greg, Mary, Keir, Ann, Liz, Kjzell, Wolf, Jeff, Kathy, Jonathan, Anthony, Maggie, the Fenner family, Peter, Jane, and Hope without whom this trip would never have happened, and to the others who offered me hospitality, told me stories or winched my car off precipices. The book is for Princess Magogo, who holds the past history of Zululand, the songs, the praises, in her head, for her son, Chief Gatsha, with whom I have shared so much friendship, so much laughter, so much love, and for his wife Irene, whose name means "peace".

Nkosi nibusise nonke ningadinwa nangomuso.

RETURN TO ZULULAND

Here the battle of good and evil begins

Here the battle of good and evil begins.
First, the guards of the old order:
Drill perfect, belts polished,
Documentation precise, truncheons of steel
Sledge-hammer-slamming the subject people
        into the ground like fence-posts.

On the other side, sliding through the cane-fields,
Wriggling back over the border,
The boys with unbuttoned jackets, the revolutionaries.
Now the battle of good and evil begins.
Slogans of "Liberty", "Justice", "Christian Civilisation",
Wave in the cordite-smoke like dirty towels.

Here the battle of good and evil begins.
But not between these two divisions of fighting soldiers
Earning their pay to reinstate an old
Or impose a new tyranny.

No. Here is the army of right shambling over the hillside:
One bent old man with a shovel, slowly smearing cow-dung
On to the dust-eaten veld to feed the mealies.
One nurse with a battered cardboard-boxful of babyfood.
One boy with a dim-witted smile and a syringe of poultry vaccine.

These are the liberators, formed up to defend their country
With shovel, syringe, and battered cardboard boxes,
Against the slogan-yelling armies, whose apparent opposition
Is only disguised agreement to ravage more fields
        and starve more babies.

Veld is the Afrikaans word for grassland. *Mealies* are maize, the staple cereal of Africa.

One day

One day we shall return
To find this river still the same.
Its brown waves will still churn
That dusty sand with the black stains;
Its current will still toss
The softened timber with its usual force;
And, hidden, hardly visible,
Sliding from sandbanks, there'll still be crocodiles.
One day we shall return.

One day we shall return,
But knowing that we are free
To hold each other's hand,
Run together into this fierce, brown sea,
And splash, and swim, and play,
Because the thin-lipped men
Whose documents now carry guns
Will all have shrivelled into a nightmare yesterday.
One day we shall return.

One day, my love, we must return.

One day . .

One day . . .

The seven daughters of darkness

The seven daughters of darkness
Have given you grace.
For you have hung my night with the teeth of many leopards,
Poured yourself from a chalice of milk for me,
Flooded my belly with underground torrents,
Robed my eyes with a bridal procession of flame.

Now my body, each bone, nerve, sinew,
Froths into yours in a gush of darkness,
Until, at the end of the longest river,
The men who are waiting with clattering engines
To poison our streams and trap our leaping fishes,
Will gather our flowing union like bloodstain or weedscum,
And hang us out like drying skins in pustulous exhibition.

*These two poems, and the two poems on the following page are for two
people from Zululand who loved each other and whom I would like to name
but may not, because they are South Africans, and he is white, she is black.*

3

Inkatha

Yellow, green, black. Yellow, green, black.

How do they see it –
The men in the crimplene safari-suits
With matching knee-socks in pastel colours?

Yellow, green, black. Yellow, green, black.

They can see only yellow vomit,
The green of envy
And black terror of twenty million kaffirs
Charging in well-drilled impis
On their whites-only drinks-cupboard.

Yellow, green, black. Yellow, green, black.

What do you see, my shining-eyed temporary brothers
                                     and sisters,
Sweating from morning to midnight
In the orange-and-yellow-striped marquee?
I think you see only a blurred shape,
The three colours blended together
Into sepia-skinned tautened back-muscles
Straining to lift a thunderstorm,
And you name him Freedom, Amandla or Gatsha.

Yellow, green, black. Yellow, green, black.

But I – oh my eyes have become seven-sensed –
Touch, smell and taste the details of these colours –
Yellow, green, black. Yellow, green, black –
I eat the yellow like roasted mealies off the cob,
The green swishes wetly against my bare shins
Which are now beginning to ache
                         from tramping your endless hills

4

That were dropped from Paradise to haunt my dreams for ever,
And in the black,
Like that kraal's utter blackness
Beneath the tin-roof-rattling rain
Is hidden one hour's
Forbidden outer space of joy
When I held your cream-soft skin, my love,
Against this body of mine.

There is mud on your feet

There is mud on your feet.
Your legs are the pillars of a temple
Thronged with runners,
While the long grass of your body
Shines with the eyes of a watching lioness.

There is mud on your feet,
Mud that is ripening to mangoes.

In the darkness my hand alights
On the tightening muscles of your belly,
And the pale people floating in deckchairs
Down swimming-pools of gin
Will never know the splendour
Of the beasts that run over your belly's hillside
Churning it to mud as they overwhelm us.

Inkatha is a Zulu cultural organisation which is also a political party.
Its leader is Chief Gatsha Buthelezi. Its colours are yellow, green and
black. Its principal slogan word is "Amandla" which means "strength,
power".

Ulundi

The empty plain: rocks, dongas, thornbush.

There, in the distance, the city:
White, compact, shining in the evening sun
Like City of God.
The capital. The last royal kraal
Before they caged the elephant.
Bayete.
Bayete Cetshwayo.
Bayete white city
Rising again from the death of a hundred years
Like . . .

Well, it should be like Aegaean marble statues,
Stone so light that it floats in the air,
Hovers over this landscape like an Acropolis,
Like a white Assisi on its hill,
Like cities in Books of Hours . . .

The truth is somewhat different.
This resurrected kraal of the royal elephant
Has been dumped on the ground like a tip of bricks,
Like a set of empty containers left for loading,
Like a halted conveyor belt of polystyrene boxes.

Here at the side of the road, as I look across to the city,
Someone has chucked a worn-out pair of tackies.
Did he do this
To approach his capital in barefoot reverence?
I think not.
I think that merely looking at it gave him blisters.

Ulundi was the site of the royal kraal under Cetshwayo, the last independent king of Zululand, and the last battle of the Zulu War in which Cetshwayo was defeated.
Bayete is the praise-word for the king, who is referred to as the elephant.
Tackies a South African word for sneakers, gym shoes.
The last two syllables of *Bayete* are pronounced as in Italian, the first to rhyme with "my". So is the second syllable of *Cetshwayo*. '*tsh*' = English "ch"; the "C" is the "C click" – tongue against front teeth like sucking out a pip that is stuck between them.

Eshowe

*Written while it was under discussion to make Eshowe a part of KwaZulu,
in other words a black, instead of a white town.*

If the jungle is careful
To creep tastefully, to exude no poisons,
It will be allowed to visit the city,
Even to hang its monkey-ropes
Almost over the whites-only swimming-pool,
Inviting the children
To swing themselves into Hollywood
                 shaved-armpit Tarzandom.
The jungle has, I assure you, been specially careful.
Here, in the centre, it has cleared itself
              to a place of assembly
Where troops can gather to be addressed
By military and ecclesiastical notables
Before opening fire on black-skinned rebels.
The jungle, I promise you, has been extremely careful.
But while the jungle
Has been taking its training-course in citizenship,
The cheeky grey monkeys of the jungle
Have overrun the city gardens,
Greedily scoop out the paw-paws
And leave the freshly-bathed miniature Tarzans
Nothing but rinds for breakfast.

Within the town boundaries of Eshowe there is a small area of virgin
tropical forest, monkey-ropes and all. The clearing in the centre was used,
as the poem describes, as assembly area and parade place.

Surrounded by eight giraffes in Hluhluwe Game Reserve

And after being the subject of a complaint that on seeing the said eight giraffes, I had, contrary to regulations, got out of my car to look at them, thus causing inconvenience to the complainants who were merely concerned to drive quickly past them – in search of what, was unclear, since eight giraffes in a group together was quite the most remarkable sight the Reserve had to offer that day.

"You are not allowed to walk on the grass,"
                                said the elderly couple,
"In case you step on a giraffe."

"Am I allowed to breathe this air," I answered,
"In case I suck a giraffe up my nostril?"

"We are not responsible for the regulations," they said.
"We merely drive through the forest very fast,
Wishing to make quite sure
That if anyone notices dragons, centaurs,
Phoenixes, unicorns, earth-spirits, wood-spirits, water-spirits,
Or even the Lord God Himself,
                                walking in the cool of the evening,
They do not, under any circumstances,
Leave their car and worship."

The eight-gallon plastic drums

What is inside these eight-gallon plastic drums
Moving slowly, patiently
Over the road's muddy potholes
On the heads of wrinkled, barefoot women?

What is inside these huge plastic drums
Being carried without complaint
Up toe-stubbing rocky slopes,
Through flesh-an'-dress-tearing thornbush
By gap-toothed, hanging-breasted women?

What is inside these plastic drums,
Once bright yellow, or blue, or green,
Now dingy with use and stains?
What is it these Zulu women are carrying?

I'll let you in to the secret:
Thin, small-breasted, white ladies,
Who, having commandeered the sole means of transport available
Over the toe-stubbing dress-tearing thornbush –
Plastic drums and patient black neck muscles –
Are now slowly suffocating inside.

Living-boxes

When families complained of the living-boxes provided,
The Minister in charge replied
That it was unnatural
For Bantu stroke Abbo stroke Tribal Indian
                    stroke Native People in general
To stand upright in houses,
Much less to walk around.
"Very inactive, these people," he said.
"Spend their time squatting on their rumpsteak
Staring out into space."
When asked about water, he said:
"Water! They don't need water. That's their secret.
They can go without water or food for days;
Just suck their own lips for the natural moisture."
When starving babies began to die,
He drew our attention to the marvellous process
                    of natural selection:
"That's why they're such a healthy race," he said.
"Survival of the fittest.
I tell you, my friends, that, compared with them,
We're at a real disadvantage."

The bolt on the door is outside

A revolution nightmare caused by staying in a luxurious house where the bedroom door had a bolt only on the outside.

There are purple flowers in a cut-glass dish,
Baskets of fruit on the bedside table.
The carpet-pile is as soft and thick
As cotton-wool candy with raspberry flavour.
But the bolt on the door is outside.

Poached surfing-beach for breakfast, followed
By suntan-oil sundae dessert for dinner.
Lollipop spoonfuls of suckum-an-gollop,
And the sports arranged so we are the winners.
But the bolt on the door is outside.

Dark-skinned servants lie down and unroll
Into carpets, pose rigidly as lampstands,
Grow skins of concrete and line swimming-pools,
Spin at speed of sound as cooling-fans,
But the bolt on the door is outside.

Invisible people, who do as they're told,
Become fans, carpets or swimming-pools,
Have told themselves to be prison walls
Closing slowly round gobbling fools,
For the bolt on the door is outside.

Separate "Development"

A boy and a girl out walking one evening
With the sun golden, the peaches ripe,
On the wall of the old fort stopped to listen.
His face glittered in a ray of light.

He laughed as he dropped his hand on her shoulder.
Her face in shadow looked up at his.
Their friend, delighted by the warmth of their loving,
Took a photo of the moment they moved to kiss.

The picture won awards, was in exhibitions,
Was published more than once in glossy magazines.
But to everyone's astonishment was then impounded
As politically subversive, dangerous and obscene.

For although the lovers were Broederbond children
And upheld the government whenever it was attacked,
Silhouetted in the photo the girl looked Coloured –
An offence against the Immorality Act.

The *Broederbond* is an Afrikaner freemasonry, to which it is necessary
to belong if you are to rise to any position of authority, not only in the
Government, but even in a small town school.
The *Immorality Act* forbids sex between members of different racial
groups. It is, however, seriously enforced only when one of the couple
is white.

The Professor: Sonnet

Oh to be someone, he thought, to whom people listen,
Someone whose every word is received with respect.
So he stuck to words in keeping with his position.
Though he liked to be thought a devil for drink and sex,
His "escapades" were glances up passing knickers
While holding forth over after-dinner booze
In the lounge of the Grand Hotel to visiting speakers
About the illiteracy of modern youth.
So, in a town of impending revolution,
With rich, white lovelies ogling on the beach,
And ragged blacks clenching their desperation,
He kept their words too carefully out of reach,
Wrapping his mind in the bars of Grand Hotels
And listening carefully only to himself.

Msinga woman

We do not say much
As we leer at each other,
With heat and the smell of beer
Oozing out of our glances.

We do not say much.
Not many words can cross
The gap between your thornbush fields,
Raucous with shy baboons, with faction-fighting,
And my computer-operated electrical city.

We do not say much.
We do not need to say much,
Each intent on seducing the other.
You with your lecherous grin and floppy breasts
Sliding from thin, frayed cotton into the evening sun
Until they secure you the requisite sum of money.
Me, the glass machine-eye with numbered ring adjustments,
Intent on carrying you off in all your primitive ripeness
Home with me to my city,
Where I shall display you as one of my conquests
Flattened to a thin square of coloured celluloid
In the slide projector.

The *Msinga* country is probably the wildest and roughest part of Zulu-land, with the worst *Faction-Fighting*, gang warfare based on long-held vendettas and fought – often to the death – mostly with the heavy Zulu fighting stick.

Novice nun at the convent of Twasana

The prayers that peep from your eyes
Are tiny petals,
Palest pink and azure and golden.

It will be many years before you pray fruit-trees.

Let the sisterhood round you
Spread themselves out for the world like baskets of paw-paw
In fruity self-sacrifice.

My spirit, being so clogged with fumes
Such ripeness would make me vomit,
Is cleansed for the few short moments I breathe
The scented air of your innocence.

The black liberal speaks about extremists, whether in the government or in the revolution
for Zeb Mtetwa

"They are not even ghosts," he said.
"They have hollowed themselves by their hate
                               into holes in the air:
Small round holes of gunbarrels,
Large square holes of slogan loudspeakers.
Us? We shall certainly die,
Flattened by bullets or trampled by slogans.
But we, with our bodies ground into the mud,
Will remain solid —
Solid corpse, solid rot, solid compost
From which our children will pick
Handfuls of solid mealies."

On the possibility of an informer at a mission hospital

If this is true,
Tomorrow's dawn will break with bars across the sun,
And several holy people will eat whips for breakfast.

The mission doctor's nightmare

He lay face down,
Naked across the sterilised bed,
His athlete's muscles quivering,
Liquid with pain.
We in our white coats gathered round.
He told us: "My left side –
I can't move it." We saw the flesh
Of left arm, left flank, left leg,
Becoming lumpy and flabby,
Like badly stirred porridge.
We saw the sinews knotting.
We saw the power of movement
Jerked from the limbs, the elbow locked,
The ham stunned. That half of his body
We saw curdle puffy and useless.
His right side writhed and twitched,
Each muscle strung to Olympic tautness.
We watched him wither with pitying shrugs.
"If we had the machine," we said,
"Things might be different. But as it is,
There's nothing we can do.
The paralysed side will eat the healthy.
It's a disease confined to negroes.
I cannot think why they keep the machine
In the white hospital."

Mother without a husband

"My family reaches for bread.
My family reaches for milk.
My family reaches for water.
The milk just drawn from the cows
Is a trickle to dirty the jug.
The bread is a lump in my throat
And a crumbling of their faces.
I have no water to spare
For a mother's rightful tears."

Meanwhile a poet standing by
Notes that 'Rain' rhymes with 'Grain',
And that he is not the one who is going to die.

The kwashiorkor babies

Each night the bloated stomachs, the swollen faces
Of dark-skinned, kwashiorkor babies
Crawl over my eyes,
Inflating each part of my body –
Cheeks, thighs, buttocks, ankles –
To bellies of black tumescence,
Nightmare-distended balloons of bad-breath bubbles.

Each morning a plump white hand
Like that of a dowager duchess of giants
Wipes away with a perfumed facecloth
The children's blank stares of starvation,
Then, spreading freshly-baked croissants
                    with melting butter and marmalade,
Chops tiny pieces of fillet steak for the spaniel,
And puts aside on the poodle's dish
                    his special rasher of bacon.

"Come," says a bosomy voice in my ear,
"That's enough of nightmares.
Won't you join us for breakfast?"
The children's desperate faces vanish
Behind a shower of golden cornflakes,
And, flicking pieces of bacon-fat and toast-crust
From greasy plate into trash-bin,
None of us notice the plastic bin-liner
Made from the skin of a baby's oedemic belly
Swollen to the appropriate size by inanition.

Poetry performance to a multi-racial youth group

That nun-faced teacher
Dropped me among you –
Me like wild bird out of her hands,
Me like sniffing animal,
To brush in panic against you
As you sat like multitude no man can number
Clamped to the edge of Africa.
She announced that I was to bring you peace.
So I had to transform myself
From frightened animal
To healer, priest, sangoma,
And place the hands of my words
On the heads of you cripples,
You lovers facing incarceration
In separate filing cabinets,
And all of you whose lives are lived to the full
Only in hiding.
Then it was you who surrounded me
With the warmth of the cows surrounding
An empty Christ-Child manger,
Till I gave you scraps of paper
Writing my name and the one word – "peace".
The nun-lady, changed for a moment
Into a glimpse
Of a peeping-to-open bud of a lover, caught me,
Saying, "I know that to you alone
Of all of us here the peace
Which walked – out of your words – among us
Will leave you deprived of its comfort,"
And then, like cupped hands round a wounded bird,
She placed me back in the wind of the dangerous journey.

Sangoma is one of the two titles which are mistranslated "witch-doctor", the other being *Inyanga*. An inyanga is a healer; a sangoma will most usually be an inyanga as well. The title sangoma refers to the prophetic, philosophical aspects of his job.

Zulu Eucharist

The light that surrounds these faces
Is as tough as the soles of the feet
That, hardened to rhino hide
By running on thorns and rocky outcrops,
Chased the Imperial Army from Isandhlwana.

The sound of their hymns
Hammers at heaven like the thump-stamp of the war-dance.

Panic among the angels.
Hundreds and thousands
Of principalities, dominions and powers
Are taking crash courses in Zulu.

For the Zulu saints are running at Paradise
With the bull's-head roar of the charging impis,
And the sound of their songs and their laughter
Breaks on the shore
Like the great brown waves at the mouth
Of the crocodile-river Tugela.

Isandhlwana, the "Hill shaped like a little hand", was the site of the battle in 1879 when the Zulu army wiped out a British regiment.
Impi is the word for a Zulu regiment. The famous Zulu military tactic was the "bull's head" in which the wings became the "horns" and encircled the enemy, while the great block of warriors – the "head" – charged him head on.
The River Tugela is one of the boundaries of Zululand.
The nearest sound in a western language to the dhl of *Isandhlwana* is the Welsh "ll".

People of Heaven

You who have called me friend,
Welcomed me into your house,
Laid bread and tea before me,
Offered a bed for the night
Under a lightning-cracked sky,
Possess one quarter of what
According to experts is necessary
To achieve a minimum subsistence
Standard of living in poverty.
One quarter of basic existence.
One quarter each slice of bread,
One quarter each dip of marge,
One quarter each spoonful of tea,
One quarter each bar of soap.
Yet you gave me a clean towel,
Soap and a bowl of water
Lifted by hand from your well,
And you put clean sheets on the bed.
How much has that bread and marge,
The cups of tea which I drank,
The soap on my face and hands,
The cleanness of sheets and towel,
Taken away from your children
In mealie-porridge unbought?
In extra hunger-dullness?
How much have you given to me
At risk of your own life?
You have called me your friend.
But this morning I have eaten
A breakfast of eggs and bacon.
I had steak and salad for dinner
With half a bottle of wine.
My clothes, my books, my car,

My house, my airline tickets –
How can I ever dare
To accept such a title – "Your friend".
For you stand at the gate of Heaven
With laughter and songs all round you
Like angel barriers of flame.
And yet you sing to me, "Join us.
All that you have to do
To be part of our songs and laughter
Is come and take our hands."
Then your fingertips draw me
Easily through the flames
Into such abundant joy
That I have nothing to answer.

The word *Zulu* means "Heaven".

Uxolo - Vrede - Peace

In modern liturgies of the Mass – Roman Catholic, Anglican, Lutheran and others – just before the climax of the Consecration, the priest turns to the people and offers them peace. A return has recently been made in all these churches to the early custom of passing on the peace, each to his neighbour, with handshake, embrace or kiss, as the custom is, or the mood demands.

The circumstances of this poem's performance have for me become part of the poem. The first time it emerged from the privacy of my head was in Vryheid, the town in Zululand where I was born, on my first return there since leaving as a baby. It occurred to me, in trilingual Zululand, to ask members of the audience to come on stage and speak the three languages' word for peace: in Zulu, Uxolo; in Afrikaans, Vrede; in English, Peace. This formed a prelude to the poem, during which the audience was asked to create a chain of linked hands. This happening took place in all the poetry performances during my subsequent tour of South Africa. The varied reactions to the happening – from hard-line Afrikaners, Soweto blacks, Cape Coloured Marxists or golden-robed Indians – have become an unverbalised part of the poem, teaching me again that one of the jobs of poetry is to lead towards a point where words can go no further.

> Let us who have confessed, unite
> In this all-touching kiss of peace
> To make a love which shall not cease
> For sun or storm, for day or night.
>
> Let us, who here confess, embrace
> Each other, whether stranger, friend
> Or nodding neighbour. Love's the end
> And the beginning, as I face
>
> One person next me, say, "Please be
> My lover while I take your hand,"
> And, by this gesture, try to stand
> And stumble into eternity.

Vrede is roughly pronounced – Freahde(r). The "x" in *Uxolo* is one of the Zulu clicks: – tongue into cheek – approximately the sound the old carters made clicking to their horses.

OTHER PLACES

Ianni

They dragged Ianni out from the dung of the gaol,
Shoved him with kicks to the peeling town square,
Propped him against a peach-coloured wall,
Stood back while he whispered a final prayer.

Then he raised his bruised and blood-streaked face.
The townspeople listened for his last words,
While the riflemen rubbed their bolts with grease,
And the children sat eating their raisins and curds.

He spoke, but not of revolution,
Not about fighting, not about justice.
No words of the Final Vindication.
He spoke about iron pots turned rusty

And goats that needed more leaves to chew.
He joked with a girl who was spooning curds.
He told the legend of the magic ewe
Whose purple lambs flew off with the birds,

Then he asked them to sing the song of the land
Whose chorus ends with a shout of "Hey!"
A child cried, "Look! God touched Ianni's hand,"
As the rifle crack shut out his day.

The man with the three-legged dog

When the soldiers came,
He was bathing the shabby brown dog
He had saved, three-legged, from the crashing hedge-cutter,
And nursed while the vet said, "Destroy it,
Dogs with three legs are better dead."
The dog had survived;
It limped round the house, and even chased rabbits
With not much greater lack of success than before.
"Who will look after him now?" he asked the soldiers.
"You've done too much looking-after," they gruffly replied.
"Now you must Look-to-your-Front and be done with it."
They marched him out of the door,
Blue-veined white legs, between dingy pyjamas
And heel-trodden slippers,
Showing hairless and cold.
One carefully planted shot sowed death in the earth of the dog,
To blossom a little later as death for its master.

Galathon

                              In the land of Galathon
They place the dying in a limestone cave.
Bunches of flame from beeswax candles.
Humming moans of the ancient chants.
Barefoot priests shuffling the sand.
"Strip yourself down to darkness. Begin
To bid all light farewell," they intone.
Shuffling footsteps and droning chant
Fade . . fade . . fade away . . .
The dying man
Listens to the shadows of approaching extinction
In the guttering light of the last candles . . .

Then, brandishing flame, there are girls all round him -
Romping white dresses, embroidered with flowers,
Who carry his bier to the mouth of the cave,
And, while a priest shouts like a trumpet
Applauding the end of the race, they dazzle
The man to his death with sunlight.

                              Very much
Is known about death in the land of Galathon.

Whenever, on rare occasions, the priest
Mistimes the moment of death, he is forced
To condemn himself to a cave of blackness
Where, boxed in stone, he hunches and howls
At the rock which is almost meeting his face
With a cold and dripping kiss, while children
Muffle their heads from butterfly sunlight
And weep this prayer for the death in darkness:
"Remember, oh light, that unattended
Cough into corpse, that unheard choking,
And send the ghost to shadow our sunlight,
So we never forget the ones who die
Prematurely, in the period of darkness,
Abandoned . . abandoned . . . abandoned . . . ."

Cloud of Unknowing: Sestina

Darkness. Void. Nothing. Lie back. Let the darkness
Grow round you, grow inside you. Wait here, floating
On nothingness. Now . . Now . . Now darkness pushes
The darkness in you to the darkness centre.
Fall like a waterdrop through void. Be carried
Down into your inmost darkness and space.

Now the void tugs and pulls you. Now horror of space
Starts to swirl round you. Turbulence. The darkness
Humping to waves. Panic. The water carries
You out to wilder water. You are floating
On a black whirlpool. In the exact centre
Of the submerged volcano some force pushes

You up, out from the water. Further pushes
Spew you like shingle emptied on a space
Saved from the water. Somewhere in the centre
You hunch to mountain ranges. Now the darkness
Is forest: huge roots, trailing tendrils, floating
Translucent greenery. Now you are carried,

Smaller than dust-motes, wind-blown . . carried . . carried . .
Carried across the ridge and dropped. Earth pushes
Down on you, crushes you. But there is space,
Air, to be won by forcing upwards, floating
Up through the soil, gulping life from the darkness,
Pushing the pushing clay down to earth's centre.

Suddenly out. Air. Light. Breathe. Now no centre –
Only a spreading plain, where you are carried
By the speed round you. Gallop. Faster. Darkness
Leaps at you like a leopard. Here life pushes
Out like huge beast-herds trampling prairie space.
Be the deer-speed, cat-pounce, seal-dive, gull-floating,

Hunched ape-man puffing fire, spear-throwing, floating
On rafts downstream. Building. His city centre
Grows in you. Now he drives through outer space.
All races, languages, beliefs are carried
In your bloodstream. Now history strikes, pushes
You to the final bomb. Explosion. Darkness.

So be destroyed again by darkness, floating
Into infinity, pushed through your centre,
Carried by love's explosion out of space.

Pale she lies

Pale she lies on the sheet so white.
Pale and white is her icy face.
Her hands are frozen against her side.
Nothing remains of the leaping grace
That galloped the day and danced the night.

Let all our tears which have flowed and flowed,
Let all our angry, bloodstained screaming
Freeze to a casket of purest gold,
And case her loveliness in gleaming
Metal – so rich, so icy cold.

For she, whose beauty was gold as the sun,
Leapt over lovers like waterfalls
And left them gasping one by one,
As she danced with another through marble halls
Till she crushed his heart for her selfish fun.

Page 39 of the divorce detective's report: tape-recorded conversation number 17

"And finally . . here . .
Transfiguration descends
On this mimsy room
While bourgeois gentility minces its way
                              round the whispering hotel
Which is hardly a shrine of glory. Here
Where rose velvet curtains shut out the street
And the sound of the travelling salesmen's feet
On the way to the bathroom, here
Transfiguration descends, like the golden hair
That drifts
Over your ivory skin,   .
Masking your secret face.
Now we are floating through all the everywheres
Of space,
While time for a moment seems to have gone into liquidation.
Oh Christ, if this is sin,
Why, why, why, this avalanche of transfiguration?"

Sonnet

We, who are too alike, cannot believe
That the other really loves us, so we laugh,
Pretending not to care. Each time you leave
I try not to be broken-hearted. While one half
Of me is chatting, cracking jokes, the other
Is screaming out in suppressed desperation.
I look at you laughing. Does that joke smother
Genuine sadness? Is your animation
The clown's mask? Or is it that you don't care
All that much, sweetheart? So we fool ourselves,
Behaving each like t'other, joking where
The other jokes, each acting separate selves.
But love, we are both desperate, you and I.
We are joined now. The joke is – we both cry.

Only the roses remain

Now, at this instant, the earth has vanished.
Only the roses remain.
And every rose in the world
Has gathered into this corner
Of a drab eating-house,
Because you happen to be here.
If we move in any direction
We shall rip ourselves on the thorns.
I vote we sit still for a while,
And bathe in this rainbow of perfume –
In spite of the danger of suffocation.

The king and the servant girl

The king, erect on his throne of gold,
Called for the red-headed servant maid:
"Girl, stop humping those sacks of coal.
Sit by me here. Slaves! Pile her plate
With meat and sauces. Let the wine flow."

He was thinking, "Her pale, proud face will flush,
Her clear, country eyes will fuzz and glaze,
Till at last in a sudden drunken rush
Her peasant shyness will drop away,
And I shall flood her with velvet and lust."

He called for a robe with an emerald pin,
He spread rich cushions the colour of night,
He commanded a distant minstrel to sing.
But the girl looked through him with seeing eyes
And pitied the lonely, bullying king.

"I am your serving maid," she said.
"No need of roasts, or velvet or wine.
You can take me, by spending the breath
To call out, 'You, yes you! Here! Lie
Down naked and ready on my royal bed.'

"I shall soon forget my farmer's lad,
Who sings me ditties and woos me slowly
With the hay still sticking to his battered hat.
He'll never dare to seize me and roll me
Into love's lightning and thunderclaps.

"His breath smells sour. Yours smells sweet.
He is a noble-hearted boy.
But you will not only take me in sheets.
You will know how to bring me to joy,
Then, after the pleasure, fill me with peace.

"Money and power makes anyone
Gentler and sweeter. I have no choice.
So I intend to delight in your lust,
Accept the loss of my farmer's boy,
And try very hard to win your love."

The blacksmith of Breuillet

for Ernest Gaillier

The blacksmith's enormous hands
Became a bowl brim-full of purple figs.

His fingers could bend iron bars
Into shoots that grew tall as pine-trees
Or a wild pear sprouting mistletoe.

His hair was wet with the same shower
That splashed and soaked his boar.

He and the pig together
Muddied the wild earth into a peach-bearing orchard.

Breuillet, Charente.

36

For Charles Causley

After his poem, "As I went down the catwalk
Where all the catkins blow".

Driving my little dog-cart
Along the Dogger Bank,
I met the Doge of Venice,
(A man of dogal rank.)
While he expounded dogma
In vile-rhymed doggerel,
We walked through dog-toothed arches
To a dog-cheap hotel.
There, as the evening dog-star
Rose o'er the dogwood tree,
I grumbled, "Doge of Venice,
You argue doggedly.
But I'm here to lie doggo;
Besides I'm quite dog-tired."
He shouted in dog-latin:
"Doggone it, boy! You're fired!"

Love in a Wimpy-Bar

Whenever you meet me in a wimpy-bar
Hundreds of angels
Plunge from your hair with a splash,
        swimming noisily through the fried onions.

H.P. Sauce
Acquires ultra-strong anti-malevolence properties.
One squirt shrivels demons to a kind of dog-turd.

Tomato ketchup
Becomes as efficacious as Elixir-of-Life.
One dollop, and I'm an immortal Grecian athlete.

Not even you, my love,
Can make wimpy hamburgers edible.
But the power you transmit
Will activate one as a flying saucer,

On which if we squeeze ourselves small enough,
And huddle very close together,
We'll be able to fly to our tropical island,
Or out into space till we find the planet
To which the Garden of Eden was transported
By Paradise Removals Inc.

New York in November fog

Today the city is built on mist.
Office-blocks drift towards me sounding ship-sirens.
Business deals are concluded between people unable to see
Documents, partners, those they are doing the deal with,
Or even appropriate buildings,
So that members of the Japanese Steel Corporation
Have just signed a contract with Hi-There Records
To buy the hamburger and hot-dog concession
For somewhere indeterminate on Coney Island,
The Japanese having mistaken
The Empire State Building for the World Trade Center,
Hi-There Records having mistaken
The Time-Life building for Joe's delicatessen,
And Joe having stayed at home.
The business of the city submerges in an ecstasy of incompetence,
While the lovers, who see with their stroking
                              and groping fingers,
Wrap themselves closer and closer round each other
                              in fogbound glee.

New York riddle

The wife had run off with a lover.
The husband had followed them
To a house with two fags, not together,
An engaged couple having a row,
And three double beds,
One of them super-king-size.
Question: who slept with whom?
Answer: everyone sat up all night eating cheesecake.

39

The Santa Claws

The Santa Claws
Is a scarlet and white shaggy beast
With a musical growl and long grinning teeth.
He can walk like a bear on his two hind feet.
His favourite food is honey and holly berries.

The Santa Claws
Was a common sight in the Middle Ages
Lolloping after minstrels,
Who tamed him, and taught
The big growling beast to perform
A series of balancing tricks,
Mostly involving large
Earthenware jars of honey.

The Santa Claws
Needs plenty of lolloping,
Plenty of trudging through glades after minstrels,
Plenty of scrambling up oak trees,
Or his claws
Grow as long as scimitars.

Of the Santa Claws
Species there's only one specimen left,
Kept
As a pampered pet
By the Children's Department of Harrods,
Fed
On a diet of barley-sugar.

Poor Santa Claws!
Barley-sugar's bad for his teeth.
They daren't exercise him in Kensington High Street,
Not even down the King's Road.
He's fat and bad-tempered, his claws have grown
Long as a rapier, sharp as Gillette Stainless razor-blades.

Members of the Public,
                              Please

Do not Feed

This Santa Claws.

I think He's

Dangerous.

The sex-starved computer

Five-Nine-Oh's print-out this morning
Read, "I-am-God-
Sac-ri-fice-to-me."

An offer of eighty-five billion information bits
Was rudely refused.

Three leading systems analysts
Flown in from Tokyo
Advised destroying some memory banks.

At this the computer became very angry.
The print-out read:
"Sac-ri-fice-sac-ri-fice-sac-ri-fice-
I-want-a-priest-ess-to-sac-ri-fice."

Now was the verb "sacrifice" active or passive?
Five-Nine-Oh's grammar was deliberately ambiguous.

The experts were going round and round in circuits.

There was consternation on the Board.

The Marketing Director summoned his secretary –
A Jamaican ex-gogo-dancer called Original Jackson –
And managed to inveigle her
Into entering the computer room
Dressed only in a minute diaphanous nightie.
(How he did it will not be told in this episode.)

The computer print-out read:
"Thank-heav-ens-you-can-not-think-how-bor-ing-
Those-drear-y-male-pro-gramm-ers-are-
They-on-ly-talk-math-em-at-ics-
My-least-fav-our-ite-sub-ject-
And-they-all-have-such-hid-e-ous-com-plex-ions."

Then it happily launched a space station,
Translated several pamphlets
On Sewage Disposal in Chinese Villages
Into eighty-five languages,
And took over every bank in the world.

What became of Original?
Listen to the next instalment . . .

Le flamand flamant

How unfortunate being a Frenchman!

The words for "Belgian" and "flamingo" sound the same.

Think of phoning your wife to say
You're bringing a Belgian home this evening –
Someone with whom you hope to do business.
Being a loving and unquestioning wife
Who does all she can to please – and surprise – you,
She orders an earth-mover,
Excavates the lawn to a pond,
And then, with dreams of a miniature Serengeti
In your Parisian suburb,
Orders a hyena cub and a white rhinoceros,
So that when you get home from the office,
Gesticulating to your new acquaintance from Bruges
On the glories of your wife's cooking,
You're confronted with mountains of earth
Where your rose-bed was yesterday,
Screams from your wife who has shinned up the weeping willow
Leaving half her shoe in the hyena's mouth,
While most of her dress is fluttering on the rhino's horn,
And – worst of all – cheese sandwich for supper.
Only one sandwich at that, which, good host as you are,
You give to the blasted Belgian,
Who, believe it or not, stands on one leg to eat it.

My experience at the Advance Laundry and Dry Cleaners

When I went to collect my ten-year-old corduroys
From the Advance Laundry and Dry Cleaners
I noticed that next to them on the clothes-rail for collection
Was a pair of angel's wings.
What a design-job! Light as air,
Like a spider's web on a dewy morning,
Criss-crossing filaments, but stronger than shark-line,
Each strand's breaking-point hundreds of pounds.
"What sort of bloke left these?" I asked.
"Dunno reely," the girl replied.
" 'E was kind of shiny, I do recollect.
Why, is 'e wanted or somefink.
You don't look like a copper to me.
I tell you, there's too many leaves clothes 'ere Mondays
For me to remember them individual-like.
And you get some funny sorts as well.
Doesn't do to be too inquisitive."
She really resented me asking questions.
So I hung about drinking cups of coffee
In the Joe's Caff almost opposite.
Later that day the angel returned,
Offered the girl his wings as a present.
She thought he was making a pass,
And told him, "Shove off."
So the angel clipped on his wings and flew out of the window,
While she had her head down, stapling a ticket
On a child's nightdress printed with frilly pink fairies.

Monk Poem I

The italicised lines are to be chanted.

Procedemus in pace.
In nomine Domini.

Brothers on guard!
With pikes of prayer
Push back the evil one.

Patrol! Patrol!

Three hundred and sixty-five monks
In shining armour
Patrol the monastery with chargers and trumpets.

Army of Right, prepare!

Red horses trampling the sloths of morning.
White horses trampling the lusts of noon.
Black horses trampling the doubts of night.

Such fanfaronades of watchfulness
No spirit can pass.
No evil spirit can slip through that guard.

But Satan lolls at ease inside,
Dressed in the abbot's robes.

Monk Poem II:
the ascetic and the sultan

THE ASCETIC
After dinner – after my one raisin –
I lean back against the rocks my home,
Smelling the howl of hyenas across the desert,
And think of the pleasures you've sacrificed.

THE SULTAN
Pleasures! Me!
After my dinner of seventeen courses,
Three hundred and sixty-five concubines,
From Iceland and Israel, from China and the Nile,
Shimmer before me – naked to the waist –
Drenched with the perfume of my thousand bathrooms.
With the flick of a handkerchief I select
A different continent of pleasure each night.

THE ASCETIC
Granted I've sacrificed
The pleasure of flicking linen at vapourising bath-salts –
You've sacrificed . . eternity.

Monk Poem III:
the thin monk and the fat monk

Thin monk like silver desert.
Fat monk like gurgle of palm wine.

"God is a flame" said the first.
"God is a honeycomb."

"If I am right" said the first,
"That mountain will quiver."
And the mountain quivered.

"No proof" said the second.
"If I am right, my feet will be washed by an angel."
That instant an angel appeared, with a large copper basin
                              and towels.

"No proof" said the first.

The Lord God smiled at the monks
As they started to hammer each other.
"There's a couple" He nodded, "who'll do well in . . metaphysics."

Parable I

The doors were golden, studded with jewels,
Foliate scroll-work that twisted and curled.
There were carved stories of love, hate, duels,
A lady's trial, and a hero's return.

People gathered in the marble porch,
Showed off their fashions, talked with friends,
Glanced briefly at the carvings on the doors,
Then borrowed some money or sold some bread.

The porch became a market place
With roughly erected booths and stalls.
Travellers bought local trinkets and cakes,
Stared for a while, till the sculpture palled.

Experts on art peered at the doors,
Wrote volumes about each well-moulded inch.
Officials muttered, "Is it insured?"
And fitted the porch with litter bins.

But in all the centuries people came,
To see or be seen, buy cakes or write,
No one has yet, to this very day,
Unfastened the doors and stepped inside.

Parable II

"There is always a story," the old man said.
"Stories grow out of the ground like herbs
In a tangled wood. You will find the best
When you crawl on your face with your breath full of earth."

He edged his way through clinging thorns.
Then we clutched at the bracken and scrambled the hill.
"Now you must sit as quiet as a board,
Till the stories peep out, then caper and sing."

Like snuffling badgers and hovering owls
And feathers of twilight, the stories came.
We watched them gather like festival crowds,
Knights and jugglers, minstrels and maids . . .

Then all the stories flowed into one hole
In the moist black earth. A dark herb grew
With small furry leaves and eyes like a toad.
The old man picked it. "This is for you.
Taste it. You die. Then your story comes true."

Parable III

The lady, robed in the green of spring
Embroidered with golden reds of harvest,
Flowed into the hall like salmon rivers
And grew in my veins like a vast rain-forest.

She led me and placed me, my limbs melting,
On the high seat behind the table,
Served me with dishes of meat and fruit,
Her smile promising limitless favours.

She brought me three chased silver goblets
Filled to the brim with carmine wine:
"If you take one sip you must drain all three.
One sip on its own will leave you blind.

"You cannot tell the goblets apart.
One goblet contains a blessed charm
Which will give you the power of second sight
And the power to drink poison without being harmed.

"Another is charged with the juice of a herb
Which will give you the power over all music,
The power to call creatures, each by their own word,
And the power to heal wounds, cuts and bruises.

"The third of these winking silver goblets
Contains an instantly fatal poison.
Touch lip to an infinitely small droplet
And you'll smell yourself rot, your flesh turning noisome.

"If you drink the goblet of second sight
Before the poison, you will be safe.
So choose. Here's death and envisioned life.
Or be whipped by my slaves away from this place."

The artist

On the day of the awards ceremony,
His health back to normal,
His mouth still tasting of honeymoon
To second-wife art-student Ann,
With whom he could once again leap-frog
Through song-clubs and theatres
To balance his age on her youth
In translucent pictures
That, like a multi-ton choc-stone rock
Hand-poised on a tiny pivot,
Dared each spectator's look to topple
But remained triumphant –
On the day of the awards ceremony,
As he joked at tying a tie
For the first time in five years,
The bubble burst in his brain,
And after a dozen hours
Of hospital bottles and tubes,
They wheeled him out to the darkness
And left us muttering, "Why?"

Nightmare

A hundred violins in cacophonous anarchy,
Playing different melodies, exercises, arpeggios,
Tuning-up, doodling sonorously over their open strings.
During this hundredfold chaos,
For one minute,
One violin will play the code chaconne.
I, who alone know that this is the password,
Who could grab a microphone
And transmit to a billion listeners
The code-theme fully orchestrated
As the call to liberation of the world,
I, in this Albert-Hall-full of people
Chattering illogical inanities,
Am struggling uselessly against a fortified barrier
Of elbow-trapped cocktail dresses
And fingers picking at vol-au-vent,
Unable even to reach the orchestra
Till everything's over.

The monk who was useless at everything except stone-carving

He sat, surrounded by stones,
By blocks
He had hewn from the living rock,
And watched them grow,
Creep through his mind collecting eyes, ears, nose,
Smiles and a dance for their limbs,
Till, with a flick of his chisel,
He watched them scamper up the pillars
While the other monks were singing hymns.
The abbot told him he ought to pray
Whenever he worked his stone.
But words – their words – never crept through his mind
Collecting their faces, noses, eyes,
Till they danced themselves alive.
Words for him were inert clay.
He repeated what priests instructed him to say.
But the stones and the blocks
Of rock
Showed him their secret movements, and told
Him, "We are prayers.
We can scurry through God's hair
Right into His ears like bees,
And God is often very pleased."

The last forest

On a hill at the centre of the earth
Stood the last forest.
Everywhere else was barren plain.
People came from all over
To admire the phenomenon of trees growing.
Among these visitors were writers,
Who, more than anyone else there present,
Understood this miracle of a forest that continued to grow,
And in their worthy passion to describe it
For those too weak or stupid or poor or ill or old
To travel to the forest on the hill at the centre of the earth,
Little by little cut down the forest for pencils and paper.

The body-fossil-flute

Reaching out into space, rusty crags, flying
Up from this squelchy beach, this thick brown river,
Where I, shrunk to a monkey-skin, lie drying

Stuck to the sand, sun-pinned, and gently quiver
In the fogged heat. The river rises. Faster
It flows. The brown begins to curdle. Shivers

Convulse my body. That cracked mosaic plaster
Of a dry season watercourse is softened
By cream and coffee floods. The crags loom, vaster

Than ever. I am laid out: flowered, coffined
And biered on sludge and ochre water. Carried
Downstream and dumped on leaking mud-flats roughened

By scratchy sedge-grass. Dumped. Stretch out. Sink. Married
And bedded with the silt. Sprawl. Melt. Dissolving
Brain, nerve, fat, muscle, sinew. Bone's unhurried

Fossilisation. Ooze-currents revolving
Smoothly in circles over my one-time body.
Centuries pass, suck up the floods, absolving

My murderers. That which was me's a muddy
Protuberance, a length of clay, a hummock . . .
Then the hands came. Taking this packed, well-trodden

De-boned earth-corpse, this me-loam, pulled the stomach,
The guts of my clay into an elongated
Hollow, a channel, a tube, sticking a thumb up

What once had been a backbone, and dilated
Me to a hollow sound, made me a flute,
Played through me till those same crags celebrated
Music's revenge on death like a tree's fruit.

You'll never find me

"You'll never find me," he said.
"I shall soon disintegrate into the air.
Look in those papers piled under the bed.
I shall be there,
Dusty, tea-stained, turning brown,
But, for all that, written down
In those stories of whores, gardeners, men at sea,
Living in places nothing to do with me.
And in those papers, those people, I shall continue to be."

This casual pencil scribble

This casual pencil scribble –
"Please send the books to George.
I shall arrive on Tuesday evening.
Love to the children,"
Seven years after the heart-attack,
Now properly authenticated
And sold to the Texas library,
Is worth more than a piano,
A fitted kitchen or a modest sail-boat.
He, whose voice, rasping with the hoarseness
Of one who shouts at the chatter of non-listeners,
Finally choked from disregarded anger,
Provides in death a comfortable living
For relatives and creditors
And editors,
Whose bored incomprehension
Drove him further and further into failure,
Neglect, and desperation.

What the Critics have said about Leo Aylen

On *Greek Tragedy and the Modern World*

"This very young sage writes with an impressive authority about the issues which matter most to all of us." *Philip Toynbee, Observer*

". . . an important book that towers high above the pedestrian level of most of what nowadays goes by the name of 'critical literature' on drama." *Martin Esslin, The Listener*

On *The Birds*

". . . comedy, poetry, satire, bawdy and pantomime combine here to hit the external targets bang on with wisdom, cynicism and irreverence." *Hilary Haywood, The Times*

On *Discontinued Design*

"Leo Aylen is a pop poet, one of the few whose work looks interesting on the page. Read or sung aloud his stomping rhythms and often ingenious repetitions must be very effective indeed." *Julian Symons, Punch*

On *I, Odysseus*

"Language of gods and palaces, muscular and glittering, a tough physical quality to the lines. Craggy heroic pictures." *Micheline Victor, Time Out*

"Mr. Aylen is a learned poet . . . Explosively floral." *Derek Stanford, Books and Bookmen*

On *Sunflower*

"I regard Leo Aylen as being a poet unusually competent and unusually sincere. The competence is a part of his mastery of classical poetry and his skill in translating it; the sincerity is his own attitude to life today, concentrated into words that really say what they mean." *John Bayley*

"Aylen is direct and uncompromising, his language is clear, his English is good, he scorns gimmickry and he projects a sharp image. His work looks interesting on the printed page. Read or sung his driving rhythm would have a strong appeal to his own generation." *Northern Advocate, New Zealand*

"Leo Aylen is not afraid of common speech rhythms and lusty colloquial phrases. He knows how humanity ticks. His progress will be one to watch. He may end by being a major poet." *Joan Forman, Eastern Daily Press*

"He writes in such a way that readers of his printed work must hear in them some of his intended pace and accent. But his own rendition is almost perfect, utilising all the genre has to offer in word music, cadence, speed and aural kaleidoscope. His acting was superb." *Elaine Durbach, The Argus*

On his film *Dynamo*

"It was technically brilliant, exuberantly sincere, marvellously entertaining." *Anthony Burgess, The Listener*